God's Working Plan to Restore the Headship of the Lord Jesus Christ over His Church

Bruce Williams

with

Alta Ada Williams

Lititz Institute Publishing Division

©2019 by Bruce and Alta Ada Williams

Published by Lititz Institute Publishing Division
PO Box 3310, Sequim WA 98382
www.lititzinstitute.org

All rights reserved. Written permission must be secured from the publisher to use or reproduce any part of this book; except for brief quotations.

Printed in the United States of America

First Edition July 2019

Library of Congress Cataloging-in-Publication Data

Williams, R. Bruce

God's Working Plan to Restore the Headship of the Lord Jesus Christ over His Church   Richard Bruce Williams
             p.   cm.

ISBN 978-1-7322869-6-2   (paperback)

1. Study of God's Revealed Problems in His Church
2. Study of how to Resolve the Problems in the Church
3. Study of How to be Led by the Spirit of God
4. Study of Growing in Spiritual Maturity
5. God's Solutions for a Spiritually Ill Church

All Scripture quotations are taken from The Authorized King James Version of the Holy Bible.

Acknowledgments

I wish to acknowledge the God of Abraham, Isaac, Jacob, and the God and Father of the Lord Jesus Christ. Without the understanding that the Holy Spirit has given to Alta Ada and me over many years, we could not have contemplated this book. During 2017 the Holy Spirit spoke to me during many nights about the problems the Church has accumulated. He then prompted me to pray for the Church to be returned to salt and light. During the actual writing of the book the Holy Spirit brought the last fifteen years of writing and Biblical research to a complete circle in showing me the topics, not our writing, we wrote about in 2007 were vital for restoration of the Church. He then showed me the parallel between the Church returning to salt and light with healing the land of Israel. I praise God's Holy Name. He is a great, marvelous, and very exciting God, a wonderful Father.

I give great thanks to Alta Ada, my recently deceased wife. We have walked together for many years. Together we grew closer to God; loving Him and feeling His love for us. I thank God for sharing Alta Ada with me for many joyful years. I thank Alta Ada for her sacrificial love for me. Her influence on my thinking, on my writing, and on my knowledge base is invaluable. This book could not have come together without her, and so her name appears on the cover.

Preface

We reveal in this book God's desires for His Church to have unity of spirit, *agapao* love between each and every one of His children, in such intensity that all have a strong feeling of belonging to each other; no matter where we are in the world.

The Church in the West is failing society, has become heavily secularized, and is losing its saltiness. God has shown to us the path back, from the current situation, to the glorious Church He has a right for us to become.

Everyone in the Body of our Lord and Savior, Jesus Christ; the only begotten son of the Father, has a responsibility to undergo the radical internal transformation the Lord desires.

This short book is an enhancement of the plan given to us by the Lord during the writing of our recent book: *The Church in Crisis,* which we published last month. The plan was described in Chapter Seven of that book. This book contains more specifics, and gives a broader overview of the plan which the Lord revealed as we were writing that book. It is in a form which can be readily adopted as an operating manual for local church bodies, and all individuals who are members of the Body of the Lord Jesus Christ: His Church.

Our hope and prayer is, that after reading this book, the path forward for each of us becomes clear; that every one of us in the Lord's body will understand their equal importance with all others, for the proper functioning of the body; and that with His help, and the committed help of each other, we can all become very pleasing to our Lord (1 Corinthians 12:12-27); being unified in spirit, not just in soul and flesh. July 1, 2019 Sequim, WA

Working under the Leadership of the Lord Jesus Christ to Restore

His Headship over His Body

Overview of the Lord's Plan to Restore His Church

The plan goal is simple, and there is only one; to restore the Lord Jesus Christ as Head of His Body, the Church. Due to pervasive, and increasing secularism, in the Lord's Body; His Headship has been severely diminished. The Lord wants this restored by His people, the Church. There are many people in local churches; only some are actually in the true Church—they are people who have been given the second birth. It is these people who make up the Body of the Lord Jesus Christ. The Lord wants His people to repent, and to come back under His Headship. He wants all of His people to learn how to do this.

The Lord has given a plan for accomplishing this goal. It involves starting in all geographic areas in the Western Nations (these are the ones suffering from severely secularized societies) two levels of local groups. These are a Local Area Committee responsible for development of, and coordination throughout a defined area, of several Small Discussion/Equipping Groups.

After you read this plan, and prayerfully meditate on it, you will see that it is the wisdom which comes down from heaven. James 3:17:

[17] But the wisdom that is from above is first **pure** (there is only one motive, and that is to support God's desires), then **peaceable** it is not aggressive, nor warring against any group; it includes all), **gentle** (it is not difficult or hard, and should be enjoyable), *and* **easy to be intreated**

(it is not rigid or unyielding; and it will be adaptable to local needs), **full of mercy** (God is offering this mercifully before His looming, and very near judgment), and **good fruits** (the results will be wonderful for all who embrace it, and for the Body of the Lord Jesus Christ), **without partiality** (no group is excluded; all are equal before the Lord), and **without hypocrisy** (it is offered honestly; with all good intent, and without guile).

It is anticipated that this structure will be temporary, lasting no more than a small number of years. Once the headship of the Lord is re-established, He will be able to coordinate His Body to accomplish His purposes. It will then be up to the Lord to bring His Church back to being the salt and light that it is called to be. He will do this if His people will conform to the intent of 2 Chronicles 7:14; a promise to the land of Israel, but, by example, applicable to the Church Body. The alternative if we, His Body, refuse to do this, is His to decide. We can know for certain that He is not pleased by the present situation. We also know what His Word says about salt that has lost its savor. He has to keep His Word; that is Who He is.

These committees, and groups are in no way to compete with local churches. It is hoped that these groups can strengthen local churches, and that leadership in these local churches will see the value in them; and promote their effort in their own church. Those who do so will be blessed.

There is going to be a lot of work ahead for the next few years. Do not worry about your age, experience, education, past problems, and fears. All of us in the Body are absolutely needed. Those who go through this effort to come under the headship of their Lord are in for a real treat, and will have a wonderfully transformed life. No one should feel unwanted, or left out. Everyone in the body is equal before the Lord, and everyone is called to this. The Body will not be complete without us all, and the loss of even one will be noticed. The work will be light for all, if all are in it. The only requirement is that a person must have been through the second birth. If there is doubt about this; leaders are available to help individuals determine their state.

This issue is very serious with the Lord; those who ignore it do so to their own peril, and the peril of those close to them in family, and geographic proximity (neighbors). The Lord has very recently spoken over His Church the words of 2 Chronicles 12, verses 1-4, 7-8, and 14. The Lord urges us to not forget the need to discern His Body. When we are given the second birth, and become a part of the Church, we are joined to each other, and the Lord, as one flesh; just as a husband and wife become one flesh. When one cell hurts; all hurt. Note that the judgment of Judah under King Jeroboam came very quickly.

1 Corinthians 12:12–14 [12] For as the body is one, and hath many members, and all the members of that one body, being many, are one body: so also *is* Christ. [13] For by one Spirit are we all baptized into one body, whether *we be* Jews or Gentiles, whether *we be* bond or free; and have been all made to drink into one Spirit. [14] For the body is not one member, but many.

Ephesians 5:31–33 [31] For this cause shall a man leave his father and mother, and shall be joined unto his wife, and they two shall be one flesh. [32] This is a great mystery: **but I speak concerning Christ and the church.** [33] Nevertheless let every one of you in particular so love his wife even as himself; and the wife *see* that she reverence *her* husband.

The Work

There are two groups to be formed in each geographic area. These are a single local area committee, and several small discussion/equipping groups. These are defined, and described, in the following pages. Working together, all those who have been given God's second birth into the spiritual realm, should individually, and without exception, work to reach all people in the Body of the Lord. Everyone should be willing to share God's concerns with friends, neighbors, and family who are in the Body. **This is not to be confused with evangelism**, but it may lead to opportunities. These groups will take responsibility to train and equip all saints in the local area, in order to restore the Headship of the Lord Jesus Christ over His Church. Membership in these groups is by invitation only. This is not a Church. The Lord separates the functions of Government and Church. This is not a non-profit organization, and it seeks no donations or gifts. It is all freely given to other people by those in the Body of the Lord. It is urgent for all to spread the Lord's plans, and concerns, to everyone they know in their local area, state, nation, and abroad. They should use written letters, telephone, email, and social media to reach out and explain the Lord's concerns, and His wishes. We all need to be gentle, and kind, in interacting with our brothers and sisters in the Lord; but, tenacious. The Lord will hold us responsible for not doing something we knew to do (Ezekiel 3:18, by example). **Every person, in the Lord's Body, should be given a free electronic copy of the book; *The Church in Crisis*, along with the website: www.lititzinstitue.org for finding more information and resources. All of us can pass these resources on freely.**

Local Area Committee Structure and Functioning

This is the committee which will develop and assist several small equipping groups, in the geographic area it chooses to be responsible for. We will address the structure, the working of, and the goals for this committee below.

Goals

To form a plan to reach, and equip, all of the members of the Body of our Lord Jesus Christ, who live in the geographic area which it can comfortably serve. The plan needs to be implemented, and continuously managed. The success needs to be continuously evaluated. The committee should benchmark for best practices with neighboring and distant localities.

Functions

1. The first thing is to adopt a name for the committee; and include equipping in the name (see Ephesians 4:12-13 below). An example would be: Church Equipping and Restoring Ministry; East Sequim (CERMES). Preferably, use a name compatible for use with an easy mnemonic. Adopt right at the beginning, a policy for doing nothing without hearing from God, so that He directs the work.

    Ephesians 4:12–13 [12] For the perfecting of the saints, for the work of the ministry, for the edifying of the body of Christ: [13] Till we all come in the unity of the faith, and of the knowledge of the Son of God, unto a perfect man, unto the measure of the stature of the fulness of Christ.

    Decide what geographic area to undertake respon-

14 Local Area Committee

sibility for; keeping in mind that eventually other groups will need to form to serve adjacent areas.

2. Initially visit each pastor in the area, take a copy of the book The Church in Crisis; or a tablet with a copy on to review with the pastor(s). Explain the ministry that the local committee is engaging in, and that it should increase church attendance. Try to get the pastor(s) interested in working cooperatively by collaborating with the equipping; by referring their people. Emphasize that this is a plan given by the Lord; and that it is not a church, or a para-church organization. It is a local group of concerned members of the Body of Christ who are organizing and administering it; in an inter-denominational manner. Pastors can seek training through www.lititzinstitute.org, in the ways of equipping saints for maturing in the Lord. The committee must not be side-tracked from the responsibility it is undertaking, and that is for it to perform the equipping. If the churches had done this properly then we would not be having all of the problems with a weakened, and declining Church. There may be a few attempts to stone-wall, at the very least, and possibly worse. The best outcome would be to have a working relationship with each church in the area.

3. Develop a plan to establish a grass-roots movement which will identify and contact every member of the Body of Christ in the area. It will be relatively easy to find one, or two people in every congregation, who are both born again and who

Local Area Committee   15

will be willing to inform people in their church about the book; The Crisis in the Church, and send copies to all in the Church. Most churches have contact information they give out to members. It may be more difficult to reach people who have been given the second birth, and who are outside the churches. One suspects that many of them know each other. After reaching a few they can then assist in that work. The Lord will be hearing our prayers about finding His people, and He will help us as we walk. It is very important to wait on Him; the quality of the results will be greater. Quantity is not the issue; that would be a world-system goal.

4. Liaise with other area committees to gain assistance, and to strengthen them (Bench-marking).

5. Provision resources and talent for the committee. It will be helpful to have intercessors, people with spiritual discernment, and prophetic people on the committee, in order to seek, and obtain, strategic direction from the Lord. People with technical knowledge in communications, especially for doing some virtual meetings; and local people with community knowledge, may be helpful. People should be chosen on the basis of their spiritual realm abilities, and not on natural realm achievements (see below).

6. Define the work so responsibilities for visiting churches, and contacting people at the grass-roots levels are all covered.

16   Local Area Committee

7. Forming a local area committee will be driven by the Lord, as He brings like-minded people together. It will only take a small number, even three or four, to start moving. These initial people may not even be best suited for continuing the work; all of us need to be open to where the Lord wants us in His Body. Scripture clearly spells out that it is Him who does the placing of His people (1 Corinthians 12:18). Leadership should be selected by the Lord's criteria. Discerning where one should be in the Body will be helpful in distributing various work among committee members.

   Consider the Scripture: Revelation 3:17–18 [17] Because thou sayest, I am rich, and increased with goods, and have need of nothing; and knowest not that thou art wretched, and miserable, and poor, and blind, and naked: [18] **I counsel thee to buy of me gold tried in the fire, that thou mayest be rich; and white raiment, that thou mayest be clothed, and *that* the shame of thy nakedness do not appear; and anoint thine eyes with eyesalve, that thou mayest see.** The Lord wants leaders who have been tried in His fire, and have been overcomers in spiritual battles. They must be pure in lifestyle; wearing spiritual white. The leaders must have trusted prophetic guidance (eye-salve). These criteria apply to leaders of small equipping groups, and to the area committee.

8. Define the number of saints in the area and use a working rule of about five percent of the total population. Make sure there are enough committee

Local Area Committee   17

members to comfortably cover the contact needs for visiting churches, and saints at the grass-roots level. This experience should not be wearying, or burdensome. That is not the Lord's yoke. If it becomes so, then revise the path. No one should be allowed to get into a situation where they are not providing family needs for time. Special members could be appointed for just this work of contacting and seeking saints to be equipped.

9. The committee will need to set up small equipping groups throughout the geographic area. Try to make them interdenominational, so far as possible in order to avoid a non-participating local church controlling that group. That would not be consistent with the Lord's heart. Leaders will need to be chosen based on the same criteria as mentioned in point seven above. Ideally more than one leader could be selected and then leaders could be rotated regularly for more people to gain this experience. Leaders will need to have been trained and mentored by those in the Local Area Committee; or by telephone or video-conferencing with mature mentors and trainers. These small groups will be where the heart of the training and mentoring takes place. Each session or meeting should involve some worship, and prayer along with all of the other expressions of the gifts of the Spirit to the Body. This is all a part of the equipping. See more detail in the paper on Small Training and Equipping Groups. Remember, always, that the Lord, Himself, will do much of the training with each person. The leaders just have to speak

18 Local Area Committee

the Scriptures over the members of these groups, and avoid using their own secular understandings. Use resources available for the actual training.

10. The Local Area Committee should monitor and mentor each small group regularly; and assist in regular reviewing to see if any changes are needed in the function of it.

11. The Local Area Committee should be in regular contact with adjacent and distant organizations for mutual assistance; and bench-marking with them to see what may help to improve the equipping of the saints and their progress toward spiritual maturity.

12. The Local Area Committee should regularly monitor its own progress toward the goal of getting all area saints equipped, and perfected. The committee should also help all Small Equipping Groups to do the same. The suggested procedure for this is described in the last section: Self-monitoring to improve the training and equipping ministry procedures.

The local oversight group should seek guidance, assistance, sharing and net-working at a regional or state level. Rules and regulations should be minimized to just those given in the Scriptures. God will provide apostles to travel to various local and regional areas to help with specific building and developing concerns. The Local Church should always be independent of other distant bodies. The only dependent relationship it should ever have is that with its head; the Lord Jesus Christ.

Local Area Committee   19

All of these points in this section are just guidelines, until saints are able to be led by the Spirit of God. Then, the reality of what the Lord does in any single situation may be different (1 Corinthians 12:5-6). There are various administrations, and operations, but there is only one goal. The goal is to re-establish the Headship of the Lord Jesus Christ over His Body, the Church. This means having all members of the Lord's Body equipped and trained for confidently communicating with Him, and obeying His individual requests of them. All must be matured to sonship, as opposed to remaining babes. A mature son can both understand, and follow his father's request. It is no different in the spiritual realm. A mature son must be able to understand the Father's requests to him, and follow them. This is what the equipping, and maturing ministry is to achieve for all saints in its area. The work has to be done in the character of the Lord Jesus Christ, and under His direction. While one is maturing there are going to be issues with the flesh; the Lord understands this. As more people reach maturity the flesh will recede.

The Local Area Committee needs to help all people grow in their taking in of the Word of God. See point 15 under the local Equipping Group. This, and obeying God are very necessary for maturing in the Lord.

Small Discussion and Equipping Group

Local Area Committees will have worked to identify leaders of these small groups. These leaders will have been selected based on the criteria in Revelation 3:18; and they will have been through appropriate training in how to be led by the Spirit of God. They will be at an early stage of practicing what they have learned with the mind; and they will still be working with God to change the structures in their heart. None of us are ever perfected in this stage of life. These leaders should still be in a mentoring situation themselves, until they have had many months of implementing what they have learned, and have achieved reasonable renewal of the spirit of their mind, and purification of their heart.

Purpose of this group

There is only one purpose, and that is to help people change from the spiritual babe state in Hebrews 5:12-14, into the mature sons and daughters of Romans 8:14. These mature saints will know how to submit to the Lord for their direction in all of their activities. They will have learned to obey the Lord in *agapao* love. They will know how to continuously fulfill the commands of the Lord, reproduced below. They will be practicing these, otherwise they will not be able to mat ure. One has to mature in order to wear the complete armor of the Lord. One has to wear the armor to safely engage in spiritual warfare.

Size, and Composition of the Group

These groups will most likely be house-based; but they should not even think of themselves as a house church. The Lord's commands to us are very simple, and there is

22   Small Equipping Group

only one goal. That is to restore communication between Him, and all parts of His body. The Lord will be able to lead His body in any direction which He chooses; after His headship is restored. Until this point, in recent Church history, leadership has been chosen using secular principles; and this is a major part of the problem the Lord is addressing. We do not want to repeat history. People who are operating in their flesh, or as a carnal believer, will come up and want to lead. The principles to qualify as a leader are outlined in Revelation 3:18; and should be followed. Being an overcomer in spiritual warfare is essential; otherwise there might be significant casualties.

The group size needs to be limited to what is comfortable in the venues available. We anticipate a maximum of ten or twelve people who will all be friends, and family. When the groups grow beyond this, a new group needs to be formed. These groups should not be comprised of just one or two local church congregations. Of the seven sins the Lord hates, the worst is sowing discord among the brethren (Proverbs 6:16-19). Denominationalism is a fruit of sowing discord among the brethren. We are all guilty of this; and that is why many are sick, and sleep early. Denominationalism fails to discern the Body of the Lord. The Lord has not revealed the steps to us about how He will kindly and gently remove denominationalism from our midst, but we can be assured that it will be along the lines of small area-wide churches serving a population of probably no more than five hundred saints. These churches would serve for larger meetings from a network of small house churches. The Lord is not likely to go against His own Word of moderation in all things. He does not want larger centralized churches with small branches in

Small Equipping Group   23

local communities (denominationalism), and He does not want small bodies who will not have fellowship in a setting where there is a full range of His spiritual gifts. When we all are walking in Romans 8:14 maturity, then we will be eligible to work under the Lord to define His future for His Body.

Group membership is by invitation only of the people supplying the venue

This group is to equip and train all people, who have been given the second birth, in how to fulfill the following Scriptures. This group is not a church, it is by invitation only, and it is not, primarily, a social group. It will be a hard-working group with one goal. The free training material is provided through the resources of a regular, for profit, business corporation. All attendees should be able, and willing, to provide their testimony of the hope within them (1 Peter 3:15).

Training and Equipping Commands

1. Take all thoughts, words, and behaviors captive for Christ (2 Corinthians 10:5).

2. Learn how to monitor out-going spirits in words, in deeds, and in held onto thoughts (Luke 6:45). Our thoughts are continuously monitored by God. A least some angels, and some evil spirits, can either intercept our thoughts, or come very close to knowing them, through their observations of us over prolonged time periods (spirit of jealousy in Numbers 5:14).

3. Be renewed in the spirit of the mind (Ephesians

4:23)

4. Be purified in the heart (Acts 15:9, and 2 Timothy 2:22)

5. Pray without ceasing (1 Thessalonians 5:17).

6. Look at all our circumstances to see what God is speaking to us (1 Thessalonians 5:18).

7. Love the Lord, our God, with all of our heart, mind, soul, and strength (Mark 12:30).

8. Obey the Lord's *rhema* to us (John 8:47 and John 14:15).

9. To be able to look at how God leads us (Proverbs 3:6, and Psalm 37:4)

10. To be able to see the pathway God is leading us on (Proverbs 4:26-27).

11. To be able to identify lusts, and desires (James 1:14-15, and Psalm 37:4).

12. To always tests spirits in all words, visions, and other sensory experiences (touch, taste, smell, position) (1 John 4:1).

13. To identify our place in the Body of the Lord Jesus Christ; and to discern His body (1 Corinthians 11:29).

14. To be perfected in love, by keeping **all** of God's Word (1 John 2:5). To eliminate all fear in our lives, in order to be perfected in love (1 John 4:18).

15. Be immersed in the Word of God, studying the en-

tire Scripture annually with a reading plan. Study it under the guidance of the Holy Spirit. This is the only pathway to maturity, discernment, discerning the Body, being perfected in love, and being led by the Spirit of God. There is no path to maturity in the Lord without this commitment. The equipping group has to help people to be established in topical studies, an annual reading plan, and using a concordance; print or electronic (easier). There is also no pathway to maturity in the Lord without being obedient to Him in all things, including commands *via* the *logos* and the *rhema* words of God (Hebrews 5:12 and John 4:34).

16. Learn to continually observe, and take captive for the Lord Jesus Christ, the way you treat all other people (Luke 6:31-38 and Matthew 25:31-46 while speaking to nations still speaks to all individuals in the nations). We can see much about the content of our own hearts when we look at these actions; just as we can by observing the words of our mouth.

There are many points, listed above, which are driven by five foundational points; 1, 3, 6, 8, and 12. As we fulfill these then the others should fall into place. As we fulfill these, then we will transition from babes to sons of the Lord.

The Lord says that we should listen to Him; just as He told the Israelites to hear Him. He also stated that His sheep will know His voice. This is basic. If we cannot do this then we have not been given the second birth. A person may be able to do this without having been given a second birth; for God can open the ears and the eyes of anyone's spirit; and does for His own purposes.

Suggested Format for meetings

1. Start by frequently reviewing what *agapao* love is, and what it accomplishes for us (1 Corinthian 13:4-13). This is the goal for our spiritual development. When we reach the state of continuing to shed God's love abroad from our heart; then, we will be completed in our Lord Jesus Christ. It is a very high mark. We need to be renewed in the spirit of our mind, purified in our heart, taking all thoughts captive, and we need to be perfected in love.

2. Share in prayer with each other and minister to each other according to the Scripture:

   1 Corinthians 14:26–33 26 How is it then, brethren? when ye come together, every one of you hath a psalm, hath a doctrine, hath a tongue, hath a revelation, hath an interpretation. Let all things be done unto edifying. 27 If any man speak in an *unknown* tongue, *let it be* by two, or at the most *by* three, and *that* by course; and let one interpret. 28 But if there be no interpreter, let him keep silence in the church; and let him speak to himself, and to God. 29 Let the prophets speak two or three, and let the other judge. 30 If *any thing* be revealed to another that sitteth by, let the first hold his peace. 31 For ye may all prophesy one by one, that all may learn, and all may be comforted. 32 And the spirits of the prophets are subject to the prophets. 33 For

Small Equipping Group 27

God is not *the author* of confusion, but of peace, as in all churches of the saints.

3. Move into the specific teaching and training for the meeting. Resources are available on YouTube, at the Lititz Institute website www.lititzinstitute.org, and *via* the Local Area Committee. It is planned in the near future to have live video-conferencing available. Schedules will be featured on the website. There will also be live phone-in meetings. Live events will require an invitation for planning purposes. These can be requested under the contact section of the website.

4. Close with thanks-giving to God, and proceed with any social activities.

5. Work closely with the Local Area Committee for help in improving all aspects of the meetings, and especially in evaluating whether the group is getting to the goal of spiritual maturity for all participants.

6. It would be possible to hold web-based virtual meetings, if a small group wished to explore this.

Resources

The website www.lititzinstitute.org will be available, for now, to coordinate and publish live event schedules; and has books and other resources available for free download. Announcements will also be made about other resources becoming available, including the start-up of the YouTube channel. This channel that will have an expanding number of teaching videos based on PowerPoint presentations,

28 Small Equipping Group

and also some based on archived live teaching. There will be frequently scheduled live questions, and discussion, sessions.

The Local Area Committee will try to provide technical support for using web-based resources such as live phone in and video-conferencing. It can also offer many other forms of support and assistance.

Other Local small groups will be a resource.

We suggest strongly that all people read the two books:

1. Watchman Nee's book: *The Normal Christian Church Life*. It should be available through Amazon, or Barnes and Noble.

2. *The Church in Crisis.* This is available for free download on the website in both pdf and epub forms. If a paperback is preferred it can be purchased through Amazon and one can see it and other books on the website. The website will transfer you to Amazon, or another on-line store.

Training for Church Leadership Groups

There are details on the website; contact Lititz Institute for more details.

Improvement Cycle 29

Procedures for self-monitoring, to improve the training and equipping ministry

For all people

1. This is an area where we can somewhat adopt the wisdom of the sons of this age (Luke 16:8).

People tend to notice things which reoccur with particular frequencies. Advertising literature has a lot of good advice, and educational literature has much to help. The main point is that when people start training for the changes God wants, they should start with an intensive overview lasting a few weeks, or so. Perhaps read the book; *The Church in Crisis*, or read *How to be Led by the Spirit of God: Maturing in the Spirit*, and watch some of the videos associated with it over the course of a month.

2. Do some follow up reviews in three, six, and twelve months; adjust the frequency to optimize the progress toward learning to relate to God, and mature in the spirit.

3. Become involved in a small group in your community; when one becomes available.

4. Join some live question sessions.

5. Self-assess for continuous improvement in your walk with our Lord. Do you really love Him more? Are you communicating well, are you having more spiritual realm/supernatural experiences, and do you have more authority talking with nonbelievers? These all would be good questions, of the many one could think to ask. If progress is not satisfactory, e-mail a question for the live sessions, seek help from small group members, and from the local area committee members.

30 Improvement Cycle

Continuously improve what we are doing. This is for individuals, area committees, and equipping groups

This should occur at all levels: Each individual should do this regularly. Each local area committee should do it at suitable intervals; perhaps every four months, and each equipping group should do it regularly.

Process for continuous improvement

The techniques for continuously improving what we are doing is another place where the sons of this age have good wisdom. This wisdom originated with God. It is good to self-evaluate constantly, and make changes when there is no improvement over time. Local group leaders should help the small groups to self-evaluate, and should self-evaluate their own performance regarding completing their task. Dr. W. Edwards Deming pioneered the PDCA cycle for continuously improving any task, or process, we are involved in.

a. Plan—what we want to do and consider target goals that seem realistic.

b. Do—start doing what we have planned.

c. Check—after a suitable time period has passed review whether short-term goals are being met (for the Local Area Committee—establish where they are in contacting people and involving them in a group, getting them reading, and participating); (for the Small Equipping Group—establish where they are in communicating with God; and whether they are growing in their understanding and ability to function in the spiritual realm. Is God opening the eyes of their spirit more frequently?)

Improvement Cycle 31

d. Act—Make changes to what is being done if you are not where you want to be; or set more realistic targets. Then go back, with any change, to the Plan phase. Keep repetitively going through the cycle; going back to Plan, after Act is completed, with the new Plan. Expertise and efficiency will both be helped by this.

Benchmark—The next steps in improvement would be to Benchmark against, *via* networking, other local areas. Are we doing as well as others, do we need to learn from others, or can we help others? The benchmarking can be done at the live video conferencing question times, and also *via* video or audio networking conferences, which Lititz Institute can sponsor.

6. Keep the ultimate goals in mind all of the time.

Rapidly spreading God's desires for His people

The social and political environment in many Western countries is changing rapidly. The moral tone in many western populations is also deteriorating rapidly. God's laws are being increasingly and more flagrantly confronted. He who formed our members in each womb, and He who created every person's work at the foundation of the world, will not accept abortion. He will be even less tolerant of rising anti-Semitism. Moves toward erosion of nations will not be supported by God just yet (the seventy God formed [Genesis 10:5], are not necessarily those present now). The evil spirits want a situation where they can rule the entire world. The less diversity there is, and the fewer governments there are, will make their objective easier to attain. They promote this concept, and incite people to attain it. We should not promote it. It will happen

32 Improvement Cycle

eventually as a part of God's judgments. He will allow it; no one is going to enjoy it. The Church should not be desiring it, for it will end the Church age, and it will end the harvest. The Church not desiring it is what God expects of His people; He wants them to intercede for mercy.

www.ingramcontent.com/pod-product-compliance
Lightning Source LLC
Chambersburg PA
CBHW061314040426
42444CB00010B/2631